The
Woman
Behind
You

PITT POETRY SERIES

Ed Ochester, Editor

The Woman Behind You

Julie Fay

University of
Pittsburgh Press

Published by the University of Pittsburgh Press, Pittsburgh, Pa. 15261
Copyright © 1998, Julie Fay
All rights reserved
Manufactured in the United States of America
Printed on acid-free paper
10 9 8 7 6 5 4 3 2 1

Library of Congress Cataloging-in-Publication data and
acknowledgments are located at the end of this book.
A CIP catalog record for this book is available from the British
Library.

The publication of this book is supported by a grant from the Pennsylvania Council on the Arts. \

for my mother Jean
for my daughter Zoë

Contents

I

My Sister's Hair

Once I saw your hair was nearly
black as mine, that your nails
grew all that time inside mother,
(you scratched your face when you were born)
I took you on. I'd sneak in, wait out
endless, boring naps and watch
your miniature eyelids
twitch their baby dreams,
breath invisible, bouquets clustered
along slate-blue walls.
Azaleas in a carousel vase.

That year, the nuns said two things:
Khrushchev would siren us to shelters
and Protestants, like mother,
would go to hell. I watched
you in your crib and sobbed.
Fat men and ugly shoes,
mothers burning in hell—
you'd never hit seven.
When I was eight I decided
to protect you from the world.

Today, going through my room
I try to hone my life down
to a few possessions. A Polaroid
of you at two, a rosary from Rome,
a swatch, slate-blue, mother used
to match her curtains, the carousel vase.
I have trouble letting go, thinking
if I save the right things,
no one will die. Your letters,
which I save, come twice a year
and once a year we sleep

face-to-face in the four-poster,
our bodies now the same length, hair spread
on pillows. We try to speak before
we dream our separate dreams. Last time,
there was in me the fluttering of someone else—
her eyes perhaps beginning to know the notion
of dreams. I'm wondering today what she would
have looked like. Dark hair? Nails?
At night I hear her silent breath.

For your birthday I want to give you
my palm. It can be gentle, pressed
against the face, or mean. Today
it's a lake that holds your face and mine.
I hold it up, hand mirror, to show
us who we are: sisters, hello, good-bye.
I want to give you a little sentence
that will make you love me
automatically, like then, a little collection
of words like a string of beads,
not to pray on but to stay safe,
to frighten away what's bad out there,
a talisman for all our lives.

Mother

1.

Mother, out of fear
you grew fat with me.
We were safe
from the war, an enemy
whose mustached accent was clear.
Father returned, injured
only enough to ground him.

No, your fear was something more
or less amorphous
Your mother had died.
You were pushing thirty
and thought a child would
protect you from what
you still can't name.

I remember your dewy Bergman eyes.
You'd stand at the mirror,
trace delicate, fleshy webs.
So I was trained
early to despise days marching by.
Next to you, I'd search
in vain, five years old,
for crow's feet, wanting
to share your sadness.

2.

Now, thirty
years later, I stay
in Barcelona, a city whose mother
is violence. She's treated like a patron saint. Today
in the *barrio gótico*

the cathedral guard
turned me away
for having bare shoulders.
Next to the cloisters
is a courtyard I visit often.
Craters within craters
pock the gray walls,
the only shrine
to the loyalists
shot mornings
before matins.
This cruelty's hard
to imagine, so I re-create
the sounds, the sharp report,
ricochet, the bursts
of smoke, how the bodies
must have folded onto cobblestones
like red blouses.

3.

Since I don't know the language
here, my world is
sounds and smells,
breakfasts on the balcony,
the coffee roaster's yard beneath.
Nostrils filled with bitter
smoke. From above, I
watch the lovely still life:
huge bean sacks lining
his garden walls, the señor sits,
fat as the filled bags,
burlap bellies, volleying
insults with a friend:

Me cago en la leche
del choacho arrugado de tu madre!
and the friend laughs.
I liked the sound of it,
recognizing the words
for *mother* and *milk*
and think *cago* must be cage.
I imagine a white rush
of doves, the stark blue sky
until I look it up:
I shit on the milk
of your mother's withered cunt.

Nights I hear him grunt
over his wife, know his fat
wet lips are at her nipples
and I think of spit, red foam
from the corners of his mouth,
his cheek resting on cobblestones.

4.

Mother, on separate sides
of the ocean we stand
before mirrors, examine
our breasts, wonder
how many years, and how many men
will touch or kiss us again
before white skin turns
gray. We fight an enemy
that has neither country nor features
when it turns toward us, silhouetted
by the dawn's absorbent light.
And it goes by many names.

The Woman Behind You

The man suspects that in every mirror
there's another, transparent woman, locked in her nakedness
—much as you may want to wake her, she won't wake up.
She fell asleep smelling a star.
—Yannis Ritsos

I start with each part removed,
scrubbed, shining like steel or baked bone.
I look in the mirror and can't see my eyes.
I see perimeter, the body's unused space,
red thumbprints behind the lids. To the glass
I say, "Your eyes are stones I want to touch
because I admire control." I rush at the face,

the noise from my throat the last signature of grief.
Eyes splinter like blue marbles boiled and dropped
into ice. Blossoms like little blue hearts
inherit my chest. Everything's so cold here,
so dry and so desperate. Stone women
suffocating the bodies they grew up in.
I always believed I'd have a child by now.

There's an outline in the air just off my belly
where a child would have been. Ever since
I was a ghost, people pass without nodding
or even briefly meeting my eyes. Once they're gone
my eyes split like glass. I am the woman
behind you, the one you think has something
important to tell.

Then what is the beaten floor?
That is my aunt.
Then what is this housepost?

A man who rips a girl apart.
And that one?
The striker of the thighs, the crusher of the little ribs.

Miniature bones piled like twigs,
tinder. Then the red behind the lids.
Bonefire. Bonfire. Beach.
I glide off granite into the night water,
float out until my friends start shouting from shore,
black bodies dancing before flames.
The way their voices scrape against the night
is what I love best, my breasts bobbing toward the moon,
belly like an airy-backed fish.
Eyes mirror the black sky. The small of my back
gets touched first; the viscous, nameless edges
lapping like a lover's tongue. I see the stars like salt,
don't know where water ends, sky begins.

Vermont

for Carl John Otis 1948–1973

Much has happened since you left.
The world is dull and people
cut their hair again
I don't like the woman I've become,
her brittle eyes. She doesn't sing
like we did then. Today, I'd like to lie
with you, reverse time, have lilacs
swallow twelve springs
so we're all back
in the big white house

we called "Sore Tooth,"
so anxious were the neighbors
to extract us. An ordinance,
a dead cat or two
could not unwedge us
from between the country store
and the congregation's church.
You, defiant Dandelion,
doctor's son.

Half past three
and the drug won't quit.
I've had it, walk out
to the green, think I've invented
in the dead of the night.
Feet attenuate: arrows. Hearts
of lilac pulse and fuse obsidian
air. I snap
a dandelion, blow seeds to stars.
Just when things start crawling
you come out to find me,

and we ease back through the seam
of sane and in
to the house, up to the brass
bed where seasons don't exist.
Hundreds of pine-panel eyes,
your purple heart hangs over us
as we taste each other's
cruel explosions, hurtle
through this black, infinite
room above our friends
until the war behind your eyes
has both our bodies seething
and we climb down
over bodies strewn
through the living room
to the kitchen's calm gold voices.

★

Still, I keep going back.
Memory suspends us there
on the green, arms like shawls
keeping off the cold night air
keeping the future at bay.
And memory spins invisible
the contradictions:
you loved my body
but fought it like the enemy;
angry at the world,
we hurt ourselves;
drug-dead,
we were brutally alive;
you wound up the hero
and the villain too; ′
you did not survive.

Even before you died,
I'd left town. We both walked
into the next decade, lost touch.
Today, I've carried myself
much further than I could
before—past the green still-life
of us, past the church
and down the hill to you.
I'm older than you now,
past thirty, one of them.
This cobalt irony of spring and
Green Mountains
presses you. Flower
I want to preserve,
how quiet you've become,
at last conforming.

The name your father
once regretted giving you
is all his own
again, yours is utterly
respectable granite, collecting
May's light. I want you here,
goddammit, to fight
with me, to fight the enemy:
these bastards who once
hated us so much
have pinned you with
the Legion's Medal-on-a-Stick.
I yank it out, lob it
into trees.

Please love, tell me
what to take to put away
this rage, to numb myself
again. Tell me what you know now
you didn't know then.
And tell me how to rid myself of you:
for years I've put your face
on other men's. Do I have to think
of your soft hair
and nails that spread
beneath my feet
to kill you off?
Will you be deader
for me then?
Tell me, tell me again,
Dandelion-gone-to-seed,
because the world's more frightening
than ever: *the stars, the stars, baby,*
we'll make it through
this endless night together.

Antrim Graveyard

Great-grandmother, New England roots me to a silence
that stretches, a mother lode
beneath this dowdy landscape.
All my life I've been told
keep quiet. But today I've come to
shatter hushed tones with flowers
for blood, for bones. Do you deserve this
regal spot, these open arms
of oak and peaceful moss?
What did you ever do but not talk?

You died when I was ten
more personage than person.
In our home movies, you click
and smile, the Queen Mother waves
to her subjects. You left us furs
and jewels. And, adding up the facts,
I see we got what you denied your daughter
who mismarried, who died before you
made amends or spoke.

What makes a woman cut off a child
who once owned her so much—
the blood given over,
the hair's shine gone?
You mutely did what your husband said
to do. Oh, Marie, I want to yank you
up and plop you down in front of me,
large doll, your best dress on
for tea. So refined you didn't even cry
the day she died.
Come, sit here. Your bones
must be cold after all these years.

Let's blow some warmth in them, breathe
so we're finally eye-to-eye.
We've all the time in the world.
Now, start slowly, silver-haired lady
groomed by all to please, kind
and kindly. Kindly speak to me.

Oregon

for Suzi Aufderheide

When you woke up that morning,
the baby was blue in the basket
you'd woven from rosewood strips
and shellacked. In the night
she stopped breathing, that's all,
the last few breaths absorbed
by wallpaper roses.

Finally, everything escapes on its own.
Grief leaves our bodies
like debris pulled out by undertow
or her humid breath which left
through the open window like a bird
deceived briefly.

Your baby's name floats
through air looking for release.
In the glass alcove, you catch light
from north and south, wait
for the humpbacks to break water
and breathe.

You told me when I was twelve and you were fifteen
to *just listen,* pressed your hand
beneath your belly. "It all comes out of here."

Our bodies respond like birds
flutter against glass, instinctive;
now the few years' difference in our ages
blends as indistinctly as the stems
that emerge out of white space
to link the roses' repeated pattern.

Cassiopeia's Chair

I meet myself walking through Grand Central Station,
but it's not what you think—she's not walking
toward me just off a train from New Jersey—
she's up on the ceiling all these years,
the Woman in the Chair, white stars constellating across
the domed turquoise sky and watching me, flat and finite,
cross the floor to Lexington Avenue.

She's been put there, it says in my *Child's Mythology*,
to teach her humility, assigned to a chair for eternity
for boasting of beauty. But how can she help
her self-love now? She has perspective which is endless.
Some days she's upside-down, others tilted sideways,
she's the girl I was at ten when infinity was easy to imagine:
light mist touching all my parts.

Now I'm numb, lacking that childhood clarity
of single-planed pain and pleasure.
She's up there and knows what's behind, beside, before her.
If I could leave my body to rejoin her and consult in whispers,
I'd return wearing pearls, mist sprayed into stars, indestructible.

Flowers

for David Wojahn

This is a love poem to our family,
such as it is. For our dog and
the colorful laundry heaped
in the closet, the seeds
I planted last week to line
the front walk. These
are what I'll come home to.
If all goes as planned,
larkspurs and foxgloves
opening little bird mouths
like an Impressionist's garden.

Last night you brought me flowers
that bled into themselves.
Dyed carnations.
You said you thought
they grew that way.
They don't.
They put the tips in colors.
I put them in a jar
and went to bed.

I read where someone said
Renoir's women were decomposing
flesh, green and purple
patches. I wasn't so vivid, but all night
felt a dissolution
or a healing. Several
times I woke, dreams
just out of memory's reach.

Last week, hairpins
in my mouth, I glimpsed
in the mirror full hips and breasts
working for someone else.

My body on its own
while I, an onlooker,
knew it had everything
and nothing to do with me.

"My women," R. said, "become so real, they seem
to give me orders. 'Bring me a glass of water,'
they say, or 'Let's go out into the garden.'"

Someone's missing from our family.
We chose names on Tuesday and
I changed my mind on Wednesday.
I don't know why. For now,
we'll call it fear. Today,
I have some flowers who
don't know their own color.

So here is how
the season ends:
one day I wake,
my gorgeous perennials all out
and in their mouths the doubt
and seeds shooting
out of their centers like stars.

Letter from Montpellier

for Hank Combellick

The impression of your words
here in this foreign city I've created
my own exile in. Always the excuses
for not writing. Always a door left open

for fast escape. Portable typewriter,
ten good books, I've rented a room in Madame Cadier's
house. High ceilings. The sound of her
granddaughter's sturdy shoes clacking parquet

makes me regret I don't have the child
you tried to talk me into keeping
one year out West. You, and not the man
whose child it was. We sat for hours

in bourboned reunion not long ago. January
and Baltimore, the gray consistency felt safe.
The town I was born in and left thereafter
you've now moved to with your woman.

Bar after bar in rowhouse basements,
we defined again scars and truths
we've always known: *write no matter what.*
Don't settle for anything less urgent

or painful than love. Love. You're brave
or stupid enough to still use the word.
I use it rarely, the men I sometimes sleep with,
never. What I wouldn't give
to have leaned and touched your face then.
What I wouldn't give to feel at ease here

with a book in the corner bar.
But a woman alone always wants something.

Perhaps. But not what they think.
It's late at night and silent as possible
in the dead of the city. The book you loaned me
propped on my knees, I touch the little ghosts

of words you wrote some distant night:
dents where you pressed hard
a page on top of this one
sure as the touch of fingertips
words like *try, idea.* Like *love.*

Toutounier

for Sue

Even the artichoke leaves
seem like friendly tongues

with their compassionate
purple grief, curled and rusty

as the taste I toast to you, Alsatian
white in the glasses you bought,

green-stemmed white globes,
six months ago. You know, sister,

being here and sisterless
has me slicing fingers not onions

when I chowder a gray-as-seaside afternoon
for comfort, try to reinvent

New England, what's passed without me
since I'm here. This time of year

the light is weak and country doors
are hung, each with a wide burst

of wild thistle
that rustles like the old woman

who hangs it, superstitious
and hopeful as we were

a year ago sitting
in the Lenox Inn

pledging loyalty to the two old ladies
we'll become, concocting our summer trip

to Europe, tossing salt toward
a future that's now past.

II

Tritogeneia: Recurrent Dream

I.

Athena under water, aquamarine
light slants her hand-on-hip
posture, one arm leans, holds up
the deep-end wall, the Olympic bottom
of the pool I swim Tuesdays, Thursdays.
She's crumbling in a line with other women—
perhaps her priestess Dew Sisters,
Medusa, maybe other versions of herself:
four statues waiting to be found
or found out, the woman of all ages
at different stages
of her life. I want to find out

who she is, this woman I
give birth to who's followed
me around for days, years.
Where was it I saw her statues
in a line, four pillars
holding up a pediment's narrative
of Greek history? The Parthenon?

I pull down the *P* and *A* Britannicas.
I was wrong. Her statue
at the Parthenon's freestanding
in the courtyard. Goddess of war
and peace, it says, her epithet:
tritogeneia: born of the water.
Also of the head: Zeus,
hearing a daughter might out-do him,
consumed his pregnant wife.
I fall asleep at thirty-two,

dream the dream again,
its refrain: oh mother underwater,

mother me, let me mother
myself, perhaps another,
do not let me crumble toward
a turquoise blue infinity
too fast. You are the one
in us all supporting silently
beneath the surface.

2.

I wanted more. I wanted less.
He wanted all of me, arms coiled
beneath my breasts nights. I never
slept well then, dreams of drowning,
of being pulled under,
seaweed, his thick arms, suffocation.
How could I have a child
with a man who consumed me,
afraid of the woman
I could give birth to?

In a photograph, I have left
him, and stand ten miles
outside Athens. Poseidon's courtyard,
one arm an arrow leaning on the column.
Drachmas in my pocket, I can buy
all I want or need right now,
a cake of feta cheese, crusty bread,
worry beads the hawker's hawk
I don't want; I've the breath
of the Aegean.

That night back in the Plaka
a black-haired man offers
me small glasses of ouzo.
We go up to the rooftop pallet,
press against the concrete, press
against night's history
of constellations, strangers
curving across the Greek night.
When he falls asleep, I pull
my legs from under him, through
the humid streets, up the hill, sister
moon keeps pace at my elbow.
We both float to the top,
and in the middle
of my life, in the middle
of the night, arched over the city,
a moment of quiet glory:

I cradle myself, rock gently, feel
Athena's ballast shift inside
like the early body of something human
ready to spring forth, fully grown
fiercely gentle, she plots strategy:
where to plant the next olive or arrow,
how to evolve war into peace,
who next to sleep inside of.

Il était une fois

Who owned anything
that afternoon?
All but one small pack—
even the man I should have

been in love with
left on the train without me.
I sat, ordered up a sweet
brown Pelforth. After all,

I could not be sadder than I could.
In the Café de la Gare
in a town called Foix
whose chateau's walls

haven't once come down since up
plain people slapped sharp cards
and there were only trains enough
to shake them once or twice.

Tired of hitchhiking
and getting nowhere
you came in and drank Pernod.
Same old story—woman left two weeks ago.

You taught me the tongue
twister: *Il était une fois
dans la ville de Foix
une marchande de foie*
time and faith and liver.

Later we toured the castle's
inside walls, towers
carved with human suffering
anyone could translate:

"Here Jean-Louis never
lost his faith." Belief
as thick as pâté
in the mouth's cave.

That night we shared a room
because it's cheaper.
Next day, diesel fumes,
roadside dances. Five hours

of grins and we still
were an attractive couple
no one would have
until a priest took us up

ten k's to a town of invalids
who'd come to springs for summer,
a whole village of bathrobes
walking slowly toward miracles.

Richard Burton died
while I was eating pastries.

Past dinner we sat
on cold pavement. Beneath
coarse concrete coursed
water. Cross-legged

in front of me, you chattered
your passion for math.
Imagine! you gushed,
fingers pursed at temples,

what the invention of it
offered the human mind!
The negative integer's
infinite promise!

And in the black French night
wined and wound
to a torpid frenzy
I almost could.

And so believing
we walked arm and arm,
a fulcrum in the damp night,
up the wide red stairs

of the Grand Hotel,
the least grand in all
of Aix-les-Thermes
and suffered the squeaks

of the sagging bed
five flights above
the sewer stink
to make

some kind of bitter love
all night to one another.
Next day, Andorra:
country wedged between two

worlds more real than itself,
a country no one's ever heard of.

Elegy for Catherine Karolyi and Georgia O'Keeffe

When I started painting the pelvis bones I was most
interested in the holes in the bones—what I saw through
them—particularly the blue from holding them up in the
sun against the sky as one is apt to do when one seems to
have more sky than earth in one's world. . . . They were
most wonderful against the Blue—that Blue that will
always be there as it is now after all man's destruction is
finished.
—Georgia O'Keeffe

I.

Withered olives on your grounds, your elegant house,
once stone barn, are what they'll contest, the best
property in Vence, the west border
a river whose banks they'd cultivate
with condos. At best, I'm ambivalent

about you. Affectionate, resentful,
I am hiding in your basement full
of photos, mice, and spiders, all lives
that carry on without you. Propped at a desk
in this once *cave,* now library, I'm sitting

on a stack of books, raised up by O'Keeffe's
ascendant bone paintings where she studies
what is missing. This week we study you
whose bones we burned to dust last week
who, when your husband died, replaced him
with a mountain of adoring artists.

2.

In Budapest in March they led you
through the theater. Dressed to beat the band,
you planned each movement for approval.
Cool at ninety-two, you watched the movie

of your life, out-starred the star playing you,
pale white flower. Such delicious, honest
illusion: the magnanimous Red Countess
with her purple eyes, wide hat, set among
applauding crowds. Your life of mirrors almost
over. Now, the orchestrated ending:
flash and pop of glass, light, sound, full-dress
uniform. Last week, I stood outside

your room and couldn't face you tubed and tied
in rubber. You were never more real
than the wide-brimmed woman you created
and, comatose, didn't have to face
her ugly truth. Loyal to the hoax, I
turned the other way to watch the honest
Mediterranean ache blue between
white curtains. Though I couldn't see it
I knew your death arrived. Your silver
ideas glittered on the late-day water.

3.

The lawyers come to seal up the house.
Shutters not once closed in fifty years
bring a shy darkness to your bric-a-brac,
your striped jacket. On the dust cover
of the book, Georgia walks back to her desert
to find the feeling of infinity
on the horizon line or just over
the next hill. Who is closer to the truth:

the woman who believes her spangled
inventions or the one who trusts what's
been there all along, amorphous as bone?

We are nothing but what we imagine
ourselves to be. Soon it will be yesterday
already. Soon I'll walk the space my body holds
away from here. I go to stand at French
doors and split myself in two reflections:

step outside to chance a meeting—
the fault of earth and sky.

1974: The Yellow Farmhouse

Daisies.
Daisies on the rue
Saint Antoine and I'm gone
—back to the summer
I burned, trying
to give up hard
drugs and see things
different, studied
Shakespeare and Love,
War in Literature, bombs
going off in my head, I
got a dog and named
her Sappho at someone's
suggestion. I grew my
underarm hair out.
I wasn't quite sure
who Sappho was but
then I went to a lecture
and found out, two women
sitting on the floral
carpet of Student Union 104
touching. My number'd
been called; if I'd been
male, I might have been
in 'Nam. Instead,
I weeded the joint garden
of the big yellow house
cabbage row, broccoli,
beans whose ringlets sucked
string stretched like tepees
from bamboo poles, read Black Elk.
In my second story
windows there were green
crocheted spiderwebs

across the corners
I'd look through
to the cornfield,
the barn across the road.
I wrote poems describing
the cornfield and the barn
across the road.
I hitchhiked
to campus everyday, the dog
still small enough to bring
and had only a bathtub
to wash my very long hair
in there were bats in
the attic there was a hill
like a shoulder
next to the house I'd climb
nothing made me happier
than that summer walking
alone with the dog
in fields full of daisies,
lace blooms, clover,
walking to the neighbors'
farm, milk whose
cream rose up
before I'd get home
and canning strawberries.
Only one thing missing:
I'd go downstairs
to the neighbors'—married
grad students, they seemed
to know everything,
taught me about lox
and bagels, Walter
Cronkite, strawberry

geraniums pinched
between fingertips
stink beautifully.

That Thursday I got a ride
with a dude who had
a van and long fuzzy
hair and who also
had a pup. He dropped
us off at the yellow farmhouse,
left, then turned around
and came back, took us
to this river he knew about.
After swimming we lay
naked on the mossy bank
and the dogs rolled all over
each other and we touched
with our hands only.
He was a painter
and always wanted to sit naked
around the house at night
in candlelight
which got me
very excited and ready.
His hair was pulled back
in a ponytail.
We never did fall in love.

I finished Shakespeare
and got my degree.
The war ended
in a year and
I wrote my first sonnet,
a take-off of "love that

well which thou must leave
e're long." So yesterday
walking the cobbles
alongside the Pompidou
Center, watching men
with semilong
hair pulled back, sleek,
close to the skull
and beautiful cheekbones,
I thought I'd like
one of those . . . one man
doesn't want to be anywhere
near me so's going to Finland
to learn the language. The other
told me don't cut one single
strand of your hair
while you're gone.
Sometimes
I just need to be able
to touch strangers
like then, trusting
reflex more than books
or words. Sometime
I'd like to be lost and found
in my own country
again believing even
without binoculars
everything has potential.
All this in daisies, day-old,
perked in a bin on rue
Saint Antoine.

Poem to Stern & Stern:
Thanks to Cousin Shimmy, I'm No Longer
Toute Seule in Gay Paree

A fresh top note, with citrusy accents and rustic notes is
sustained by the emphatic warmth of spices. Enhancing
the rush of spices is a floral nuance which adds to the
fragrance's refinement. The harmonious accord of spices
and flowers expands on a woodsy background reinforced
by amber and musky overtones.

—*Ominum de la Parfumerie de Luxe, Tsar cologne*

Yesterday while M. was at the Les-Gay march
(they wound up meeting on a barge, champagne,
caviar, the Seine—should I have gone?) you read,
David, the poetry of perfumes while,
Jerry, you gave me the booty of your
visit: a bag of miniature colognes
—two each—that cousin Shimmy gave you.
So I wanted to write you both a note
this morning, having just spent the night with Paco.
I know, I know, you told me to give it
to the man in my life, but since there's none
at present I had to play both parts.
We went to bed and dreamed Liz's *Passion*.
At this very moment her little desk-size
portrait smiles at me—purple eyes, purple nails,
purple vial. While you whisked off to perfumeland
this A.M. (Grasse, Nice), I applied
the ultra-light crème guaranteeing
a "super-protective day." They say it
"neutralizes the effect of free radicals and light rays,"
so this must mean whatever of you
may have rubbed off on me will be gone
by nightfall. I'll have to apply the "jeunesse"
promised by the stuff called Stendhal and pass

the evening writing my red and black
childhood. When bedtime rolls around again
I'll try the firming crème and have a choice
of scents—Tsar, Georgio, or
(they're three of these) Paco, Paco, Paco.

Bicentennial Bastille

for Marilyn Hacker

The emblem of the week and month and year
is birds in flight. They stand for freedom, rights
of man. Renaud, the protest singer,
redesigned the logo so the flight's
of MIG jets, not birds, the words *ça suffat
comme ci* (he often twists the words around)
emblazoned underneath and then *apar-
theid, debt,* and *colonies.* Last week, around
Bastille's tall green column, the Third World
rallied: Nicaragua, Palestine,
Nouvelle Caledonia, banners unfurled
and carried through the streets, solidarity lined
up for miles. Meetings at Mutualité
followed. This week, the Grand Septs' banalities

as today, the chiefs of state held their meeting.
That is, the chiefs of states of industry.
The poorer ones don't count. Friday, leading
the first string in a round of smiles—crusty
Mitterrand. George and Maggie flanked him.
Next to them the other ones—the Kraut,
the Wop, the Jap, Kanuck—all there to thank him
for his hospitality. Inside the out-
side-letting-in pyramid (which can't be said
of the Grand Sept group) hot air rose
and steamed the glass. Past Pei's peak, the dread
blimp—the fattest spy there ever was—
wheezed, nosed above the streets of Paris,
security-secured to snare us

unsavory characters in the mob
which Thursday stormed the Bastille Opera.

Exotic glass wings, it nests on the cob-
bled *place.* Opening night. Paparazzi
perched on the mezzanine with distinguished
guests. Helicopters rested below like dogs
outside a store. The *citoyens,* squished,
celebrated, lost their heads, wine-ideologues,
charged the streets with firecrackers, danced in red caps,
spiked hair, frilled bonnets, sang *La Marseillaise.*
We walked the peppery streets, found a café,
round table. Seven people, seven countries,
sounded off names, places, and professions—
the little peoples' summit was in session.

"Of course he's an opportunist despot,"
says José of Noriega, "but at least
he thinks of Panama—despite
what you say—as a *nation*—diseased
mainly by those who twist it as a nut or bolt
in America's industrial machine."
"The rights of man, indeed! What rot!"
fumes Gerry, "What about the mine
workers and Maggie's might?" "It's by crushing
the backs of the oppressed the Big Guys make
their bucks," Daniella says. Then we're discussing
more important issues: Green Party's slate,
what do Scotsmen really wear beneath their kilts?
"State secret!" states Gerry, pissed to the gills.

The pivotal *spectacle* was the *défilé*
arranged by "uncle's" flashy ad-biz man—
miners, pipers, pom-poms on parade
in an attempt to outglitz rich Uncle Sam's

Miss Liberty event. Elysian surreal.
Zebras weren't zebras but horses painted striped.
A train slipped through a blizzard of soap peels.
Miners were actors hired for the night.
When Jessye Norman sang *La Marseillaise*
crocodiles might've envied her ersatz tears.
Draped in an oversized French flag, arm raised,
she torchsonged France's last two hundred years.
At La Concorde, in-Paris Americans
boogied to James Brown instead of Gershwin.

The blimp buzzes over us, June bug in
July. We're here to see the sky explode
fireworks, hope to get a view, snug in
the Marais, far away from crowds.
Gazing up, "a royal blue aquarium,"
you say, "the blimp looks like a whale." It floats
past the flag raised by an American
on his penthouse terrace. It floats
past the sharpest spire of Notre Dame
and—doesn't pop! Fireworks do,
bubble up from Trocadero. "Damn!"
I say, "if we were rich we'd have a view."
Instead, a flock of doves catches light—
embroidered white blossoms on a velvet night.

Christmas Card from Vence, France

for Laszlo

But the silent violins now emerge,
And like the big wing of a bird, smother everything
In a darkness from which only a single horn escapes—
That feels effaced by the composer's dream . . .
But he is not dreaming,
The composer is finishing two performances simultaneously!
—Norman Dubie, "The Composer's Winter Dream"

I

Winter is emerging and I am
collecting gifts to give:
hollowed eggs gently painted,
an art of hands and eye,
balance of a fragile world
nearly lost. I watch the snow

(still rain down here)
descend the mountain
like a husky, white-furred
trapper moving through the woods
toward another century
into a clearing, a cabin,
a fire inside. That's how

it happened. But it was summer
when out of nowhere
or, more precisely, out
of the woods he dropped
down the steep path
looking for something
he'd lost. I was

45

gathering rosemary
on my terrace and stood;
the spicy crescents
fell at my feet. I knew
I was a goner
when he said later

they reminded him of Balaton,
the garden, his grandfather
whose nails he'd cut,
the old Magyar too old
and too feeble. Call him

a throwback or old-fashioned,
but think of me in love
with a gentle man,
a rush of silent violins
each time he touches me.

II

We agree our future
child will play piano.

He composes the dream
on my stomach, taps
large fingers
on that egg-smooth surface.

I tell him to tell me
something he's never said
out loud. "When I was four," he says,
"my father soaped
my hands in his, surrounded them

completely, a happiness
as large and safe as that
I'd never known before."

III

Looking for something
with neither shape nor sound,
his father left.
And so did mine.

Did they ever find it?

"Do you see yours anymore?"
I ask, but he's asleep.

I move toward his dreams
and find my face fits perfectly
between his shoulder blades

like continents that drift
apart, then back again
together.

Christmas Shopping in Venice

He didn't really like travel, of course. He liked the idea of
travel, and the memory of travel, but not travel itself.
—Julian Barnes

Is there anyone but must repress a secret thrill, on arriving
in Venice for the first time and stepping into a Venetian
gondola? That singular conveyance, come down un-
changed from ballad times, black as nothing else on earth
except a coffin.
—Thomas Mann

Everything's like opera with the fog.
We're supposedly ecstatically in love
and waltz through the chamber of the doge's
council and you hug me too hard and I
bite you like a dog. Your anger scales
to the colossal figures on the wall:

Tintoretto's *Paradise*. I apologize,
apologize, and laugh. You stride off
through St. Mark mist and I stomp down beneath
the Bridge of Sighs. *Jeezusss Criiminy*
my mother used to say. I'm waiting for you
back in the hotel, and listen to the lack

of traffic, wonder how adults can act
so stupid, fall asleep reading Tintoretto's
journals; his angels hung on wire,
swinging through gray Venetian space,
foreshortened ecstasy. At five, bells strike
me awake in the prime of my life

in the middle of Venice and I'll be damned
if I'll wait in the room for you to come back.
(You're out there publicly despising me.)

I hit the streets. How lovely the smooth
fog and the smooth necks of the sailors!
How easily they understand each other,

gossiping and gliding over bridges,
never lost, their ankle-length capes pneumatic
triangles. I wander past the windowed shops,
masks and riches, east and west, past dross
of daily lives that floats in slick
canals. Everything's banal. Even gondolas

seem dark, rotten bananas. Wasn't Auschenbach's
last step his first toward uncompromised
beauty? I'm dead-ended at the Grand Canal,
must go back, re-trace steps, until
I know: it's getting lost this visit's
all about. I *vaporetto* to the palace,

reuse this morning's ticket and pace
with cold feet the dark walls, hold a mirror
to study ceilings: apotheosis
of the loved one: everyone sweeps toward
heaven with that easy urgency
Tintoretto's caught, divine *because*

they're flawed, not in spite of. In the last
light of day I walk down the Giants' Stairs
and there, through dusk, foreshortened,
you are. Hallelujahs have us walking
through the streets, piped music for Christmas
shoppers and bowers of white branches

crowds and cries of babies, fathers' well-dressed
gossip, glass beads, glittered masks eye us

and we're just in time to watch the hour strike:
the giant Moors pound it out high above us
in Saint Mark's. We hold each other up
imperfectly beneath time's tower:
all around us the spectacle of pigeons
rushes toward, away, and with the sound.

Sicilian Sestets at Etna

There is nothing left on earth that's new
so we repeat old stories, journey
like a million others, commit the same
limp mistakes, take ourselves where we can
trace the folly of someone else's life
and feel superior, Queen/King-for-a-Day.

We are modern—so we know there's no
such thing as gods with little g's,
deities they once raised and razed towns for.
Wave Maker and Earth Mother palling around
in the clouds. We know it isn't true—
we have astronauts and atom bombs to prove it.

Even so, we went there. And we saw the mountain
steaming like a pot. A lot of fuss
and people climbing in slow Jeep-loads
up the slopes, hauling their small rituals
of automatic cameras. Against all odds
of being heard, they threw their scrappy voices

to the wind. And the mountain ate them hungrily.
We took away whatever morsel of belief
we might have found, six remembrances
of lava, and descended to the crescent-shaped
theater where Greek voices rose like flags
of steam past turquoise sea and purple Etna.

Later in the water, far removed from shore
but shallow nonetheless, I Demeter
your Poseidon: nothing's impossible,
you said, sliding slowly into me,
and I was more and more receptive
to making love at half the normal weight

and we whirled clumsily at first against
the water's physics, till we formed our own
orbit, gravity, laughing back to that
original home in water's outer space
and face to face came gloriously
to all those other ancient, made-up lives.

Winter Garden

for Ann and Sophie

The day you gave birth
a man who'd had a nervous
breakdown five years
earlier was showing me
his cellar: around us
garlic tresses
hissed, groomed and crisp,
holding their cargo inward,
as you and I have traveled through
years, countries, and lovers,
exotic lives looking for
real love or what
would make us not ordinary.

In June we sat on the bluff
of the wild Pacific
wondered were we
the stuff mothers are made of
then walked through the brown fields,
watched cows, found lupine, poppies
beneath weeds, protected.

The day you gave birth
was night here and deep
in a Jura mountain
the man said first
he'd followed directions,
dug deep, placed each bulb
such and such
and so and so
in special crates.
But they grow
anyway, no special care,

and anywhere—
plastic buckets, old cracked bowls,
unused corners. His subterranean field
healed him, hundreds
of fat pale tongues that stuck
black air, the missus' three
varieties of cherries, ketchup spiced
with anise.

For years now,
home's where I am and I am neither
here nor *there*.
Settled in
their ceremonies of bread and tea
late evening fires, they fed me
three days, and I slept
under puffed white comfort,
a high room,
lace curtains.

The night you gave birth (your day)
I woke, endives deep below
two stories
squeaking tender bodies,
the hint of green.

Ten fingers and toes,
how the perfectly
simple can sometimes save us,
the strange turns ordinary,
the ordinary, exotic:
the coronet of bread
that fills my rear window
on my way home.

III

★

Stereograph: 1903

She means two things
and leans on the gentleman's
right arm. All these years.
These two decided
to take a walk

or a boat ride. After a while
they sat down, discussed
the weather. And the tide
changed. Now they sit
above the title,
"Waiting for the Tide."

When I was nine, I waited for the girl
who looked just like me,
talked and did everything the same
at the same time. Our meeting
would take place at Compo Beach
both of us wearing our green plaid suit.

We'd sit down and face the water,
explanations unnecessary. Then
both rise and walk
into the other's territory.
Her mother was perfect—
the one who runs to me,
great concern on her face,
holding in her arms,
all the years
I've imagined her.

She gives me the gift
of this antique viewing card,
one side's almost-identical

twin pasted next to it
for someone's drawing room pleasure.

Suddenly the two women rise, walk
into the background, the woods,
arms around each other's waist.

Traveling

We have spent this trip
now nearly over
visiting dark places, each other.
We will always be
mother and daughter
but finally are two women
conversing at dinner.

I've taught you words
pain, coeur, as you once taught
me, your voice a reassuring night-light
I'd forgotten. Last night
you undressed and your body's
lovely silvering swam in moonlight.
That I've seen you
naked for the first time
in years tells me
as it did then
what beauty is to come.

High in the mountains
we go into Romanesque dark.
The Virgin pulls back her robe,
coy, reveals her idol's heart,
ringed in forget-me-nots.
I scratch moist walls, residue
under nails. Our steps drip
toward a solitary ruby
votive. Far above the rest
of the world, you say
after you're gone you want
a single candle like this
mountain church's.

Outside, light crashes
over us as it did when we'd run
into mad Atlantic breakers
mother and child
hands locked for safety.

The Night Before

The night before
your surgery, a storm
left a tiny sand island
just off shore,
invisible the day before.

I slept with you
and we listened
to the storm unfurl
sure and urgent and
tried not to speak
of the "one small spot,"
they'd come across by accident.

You tossed all night
like a wave
that doesn't know how
or where to go.

Next morning, mother
and three daughters
walked and came upon an island
where no one's ever stood.

It hadn't been before.

We danced, we four
chanted, claimed
and named the island
after all of us,
a kind of superstition
I suppose, thinking
if something that soft
could hold us up,

and love our bare feet
like a human palm,
we'd be saved.
Next day
it was gone.

October: La Madonne de la Fenestre

October now, it must be
snowing at that dead end
where mountains' cupped hands
held us up to sky.

Here, a surprise snow
I watch from your hospital
window as I pluck dead blossoms
from plants that crowd the sill.

What aches as much as anything
is the ruse of only weeks ago:
you and I walking goat paths in the Alps
And we didn't know. And we didn't know.

We mused over cows' comic
gravity: How could they hold on
to slopes *that* steep
and not fall off?

Arms damp with cloud
we stopped into the village shop
and asked where we'd find wintergrün.
It brings good luck

said the woman in her fine patois
but you've got to leave the path
to find them. We settled for the weedy
digitalis, wild foxglove.

It wouldn't give at first.
I used my knife. Loose blossoms
fell to earth before the stalk
gave way. We walked a ways

beside the water-rush
so loud we couldn't hear our voices.
Mother, it's surely snowing
in that cul-de-sac of earth.

Summer's growth bends
and with it our voices,
trapped in that moment
with the weight of seasons coming on.

I imagine a woman there
upon whose face I've put
the silent joy
we shared in August.

Though her spells are strong
she cannot stop the water.
She hesitates before she climbs
where no path goes.

The Night of Your Funeral

after three months'
preparation, the day's
ceremony, a hundred or so
people to console,

after the hollowed out
purple cabbage filled
with tasteless dip
was put away
and turkey, ham, and beef,

after the polite talk—
your brother's
two wives (ex and new)—

and after all
the photographs
and tales of you
were swapped

and your other two
daughters and your son
went home to bed,

I came home
to yours
(mine too far away),

to your absence
to the clatter and clamor finished
to your brush, your hair,
to your face, your mirror

to your robe
and climbed in
your bed again

and then all I had
of you ·
was me.

Cindy,

I'm sending you this rose
flat and flaky
which spent its last season
pressed between *blessed* and *blasphemy*
in the dictionary, words
that sleep on top of each other
every night. Imagine
the flower filling with air
and becoming a balloon
that takes you
away from these difficult days
the heat, your body
that's still an enemy
when you thought at least
by now you'd have it
to call yours again
and the perfect
boy child you brought home
last week screams
no matter what.

What a conspiracy,
this misty-motherhood business,
soft breasts and lace!
Your breasts itch, leak,
tough spouts that wake you,
after three hours' sleep
and you pace, pace, motherhood's
no breeze on a hot, humid night
and your mother
who might at least
have warned you
died on you.
Your guilt stands

at the window waiting
for answers
or absolution.

The baby we call "Jaws"
is asleep. You lay him down
and his triangle mouth
makes you think
one more day,
I can handle one more.
The advice she always gave us.

Santorini Daughter

for Ann Elliott

Mother, blood irises unfold
beneath the window. I sit
all night, movement undetectable.
You climb through a window to a past
where you're healthy again, gathering
sheets so they settle
like limp white birds
in the straw hamper.
You scrub them at the village
basin, your voice purling
with the others', then hang
the sheets like sails
that slash the blue ocean.

It's morning and you're
awake and dying in the room
where you gave birth to me;
outside, our cobbled streets
surge downhill to sea.
I must ask you questions,
not to continue the stifled
red voices of our women.
If at any time you're in pain
please tell me. To explain

your life, you climb off the bed and
pull back the gauze curtain,
your arm curved and voluptuous
to me for the first time.

Out the window the white walls
bend down to the Aegean.
My first memory is of these
contrasts: blue and white,
men at checkers, women at water.
Old women glide in black shawls
through the windows, the white rooms
heads slightly tilted
as though just about to ask
questions. One looks birdlike
and delicate. The others
carry locks of hair reminding
us what ugly children we were.
How they hoped to turn us
into wonders, exotic butterflies!

At times I wonder how there's
life in a place where there are
only white houses round as shoulders
cutting into the sky and ocean,
everything's so still. Below the window
they're already keening. A woman
I don't recognize is just coming
around the corner, her arm curved
over a rough basket. She reminds
me of you. Oh, if only I could see
what's inside her basket.

The Mother of Andromeda

It's been years since we left Ethiopia
and I can still smell the seaweed ripe and hot
in the rocks near Joppa where she was chained.

At first, she complained, which made her no less
beautiful: that liquid hair I'd want
to get my tongue around it seemed so sweet,

the flesh that made me melt with pride. Those eyes,
they were the very meaning of life.
How we'd whisper in the old days, heads

at dawn like two conspirators' touching
on silk pillows until we had to rise,
keep others' company. She grew, as all girls do,

and grew away from me, but came back, always
with her questions. And then those tattletale
Nereids had to wreck it all. My name

alone runs red as berry juice, the tea
we'd brew and sweeten to get cool. Cassia,
cassia-juice, Cassiopeia. My daughter,

chains hissing at her wrists like alarms
to passing Perseus: was it love at first sight
or common courtesy when he saw

the serpent slither greenly and far too
sexy for his own damn good near my naked girl?
Whatever. He pulled Medusa's charmed

and severed head from his bag of traveling tricks
and that was that. The rest, they say, is history.
The headlines read: *man with flying sandals*

turns attacker back. Gets the girl.
He's not the son-in-law I would have chosen.
And she, still with grit between her teeth and toes.

Last night, from here, I saw you down below
look up at us and wonder who we were:
the monster, my daughter, my loyal husband, and the rest
turning through infinity above your sleeping heads.

Dream, July 10

In the dream, I'm choosing
whether to live or not. There's
a little chart on the wall
like a target. I've checked out
of the hospital, fed up
with institutions. My mother
stands tall and healthy
and is happy to welcome me
to the other side. My sister, urgent,
says decide, decide, you're
not covered and you're
costing us a fortune
in daily rates.
Mother picks up a white ball
which turns into a kitten
and says *see, see how soft?*
I think of taking it
though all my life
I've hated cats.
How I miss her.

When I wake
it's my sister's birthday.
Later, I telephone overseas
and every time she tries
to be the listener,
the one-who-understands, *there there,*
I change the subject.
Her baby son
knows more than they suspect:
Tuesday, presented to a photo
on the wall of all of us,
he pointed to his dead grandmother
and me, both of us
absences in his life.

73

Prisms

Eight months since your death,
my study's full of light
and I'm studying French: *pélérinage*—
the old village
we climbed through
last year marked
the middle of nowhere
one point on the long, worn
path that leads to Spain.

Your life ended just like that,
abrupt, nothing
to explain it but faith
and hard, plain biology.

I understand nothing
I said to you
when we passed the chapel door
and three old women
in mild debate, quaking
leaves of linden trees,
dappled light.

There you go,
a surprise of rainbows
infuses the room
—the heart-shaped prism
once in your window
now mine, sheds its color,
sings silence everywhere.
It's how I see you now,
soft and complicated light,

here and not here.
I put my hands into
the colors
of your voice
and they sift, weightless
through our fingers.

Havasupai Woman

Decision isn't in her
language. And no word
for the division of time,
so everything happens at once.
A child is growing in me
and the Supai woman
all night scrambles
canyon walls like maidenhair fern,
dances circles, glances
at the Wegaleva god and goddess
who'll someday topple
and take the Havasupai people home.
There's comfort knowing
you've no choice.

She darts to
the circle's center. The heart. Drums.
Pulls her hair, dashes at
the center post, a wrinkled crone.
One night they surround her, wrapped in doeskin, a pregnant
woman can prevent rain or bring it on.

Last night soft as dawn she says
looking right at me:
talk to coyote,
scratch yourself with a manzanita stick,
if you want to get rid of it.
If it stays after that
you'll keep it
and paint dried umbilical cord,
ochre Vs on the forehead
so it will know who it is.
I walk toward her,

standing at the falls' edge,
her whole body gathering
to the naked brown dive
into the blue-green pool.
She turns to stone, red
as the shape of love.

I wake
believing in forms,
in everything I hear
or see
and dream.

Notes

"The Woman Behind You": The italicized lines in the
poem are from the Venda hut-naming ceremony of
"Language Event II," in *Technicians of the Sacred,* ed.
Jerome Rothenberg (Anchor Books, 1968).

"Toutounier" remembers Collette's story by that name.

"Elegy for Catherine Karolyi and Georgia O'Keeffe":
Catherine Karolyi died in 1985, as did Georgia O'Keeffe.
She was the widow of Michael Karolyi, Hungary's
socialist president from 1955 to 1956 and founded in his
memory the Michael Karolyi Foundation, an artists'
colony in Vence, France. O'Keeffe's remarks are from the
exhibition catalogue, "An American Place" (1944), and
quoted in *Georgia O'Keeffe* (Viking Press, 1976).

Acknowledgments

My sincerest thanks go to Marilyn Hacker, Joe David
Bellamy, Debra Kang Dean, Gay Wilentz, Lynne Frye, and
Mary Carroll-Hackett for their reading of this manu-
script, to Lillian Robinson and Jeff Franklin for their
biweekly insight and audience, to William Ashworth for
touring me through celestial maps, to Marc Vinsant for
his *mots justes,* to Ita Roberts, and most especially to Ed
Ochester for his belief in this book. I am very grateful
also to the North Carolina Arts Council, to the
Macdowell Colony, the Virginia Center for the Arts, the
Millay Colony, the Tyrone Guthrie Centre, the Michael
Karolyi Foundation, and to East Carolina University's
College of Arts and Sciences, Department of English, and
Research and Creative Activity Committee, for grants
and fellowships that have allowed me the time and means
to complete many of these poems.

Acknowledgment is made to the following publications
in which some of these poems or versions of them
appeared: *The Feminist Renaissance, Genre, Gettysburg
Review, Manhattan Poetry Review, Mountain Newsreal, New
Letters, Oxford Magazine, Ploughshares, Prairie Schooner,
Primavera, Puerto del Sol, Shenandoah, 13th Moon,* the
Women's Review of Books.

"The Woman Behind You" appeared under the title, "In
Every Mirror" in the chapbook *In Every Mirror* (Owl
Creek Press, 1985).

Photo by Henry Stindt

Julie Fay grew up primarily in southern New England. She is the author of *Portraits of Women* (1991), a collection of poetry, and she teaches writing and literature at East Carolina University, splitting her time between Blount's Creek, North Carolina, and Montpeyroux, France.

Library of Congress Cataloging-in-Publication Data

Fay, Julie.
    The woman behind you / Julie Fay.
        p.   cm. — (Pitt poetry series)
    ISBN 0-8229-4082-5 (acid-free paper)
    ISBN 0-8229-5682-9 (pbk. : acid-free paper)
    1. Feminism—Poetry. 2. Women—Poetry. I. Title. II. Series.
    PS3556.A9944 W66 1998
    811'.54—ddc21   98-25469